To my mom, what burped me

—A.B.

To all the kids (and kids at heart)
who appreciate a good fart joke

—P.T.N.

Text copyright © 2014, 2025 by Artie Bennett Illustrations copyright © 2014, 2025 by Pranas T. Naujokaitis
All rights reserved CIP data is available First published in the United States 2014 by
Blue Apple Books, South Orange, New Jersey www.blueapplebooks.com
Art Direction and Design by Elliot Kreloff

Artie Bennett

illustrations by Pranas T. Naujokaitis

BLUE APPLE

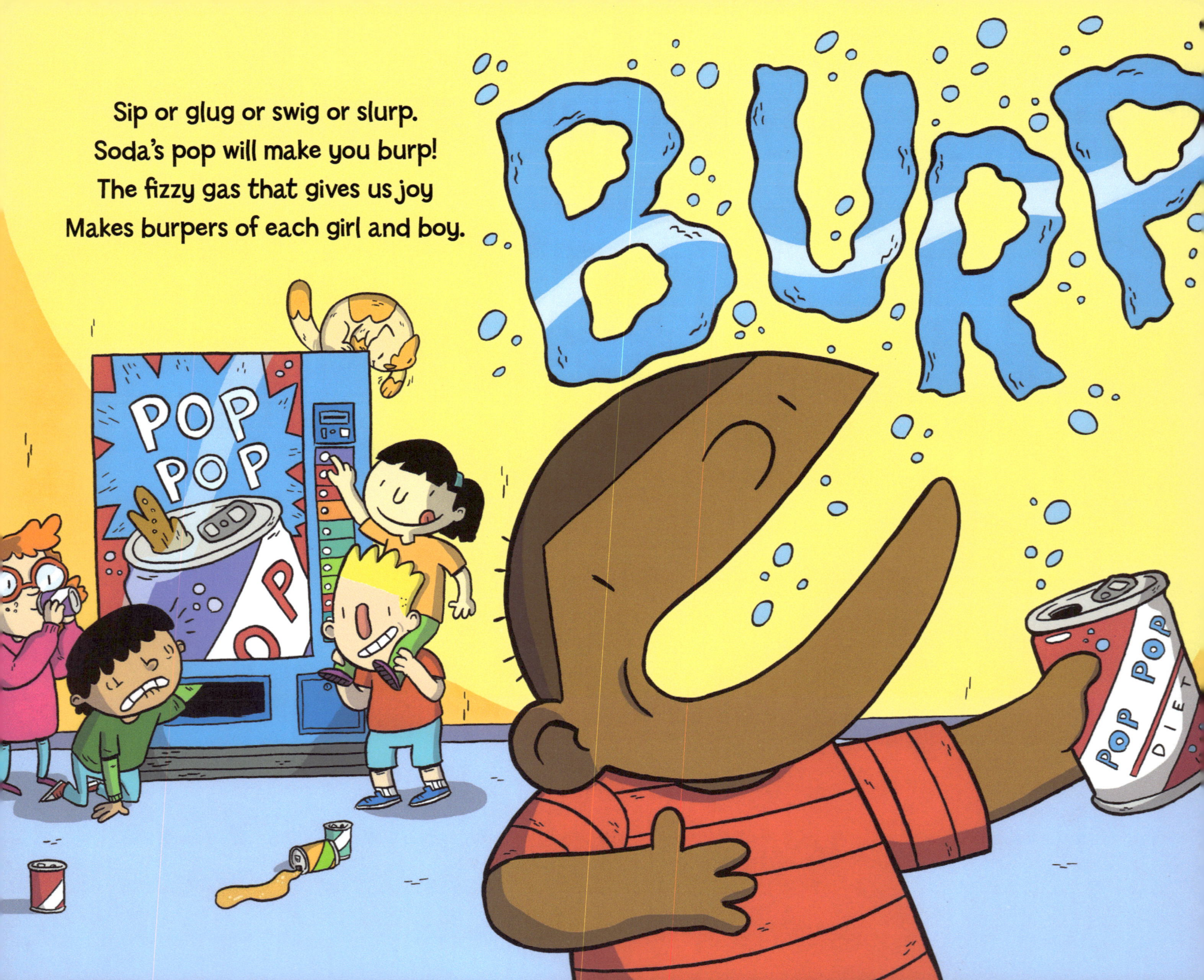

Burps are sometimes barely heard

Or loud as any mockingbird!

Here's one of nature's stranger facts:

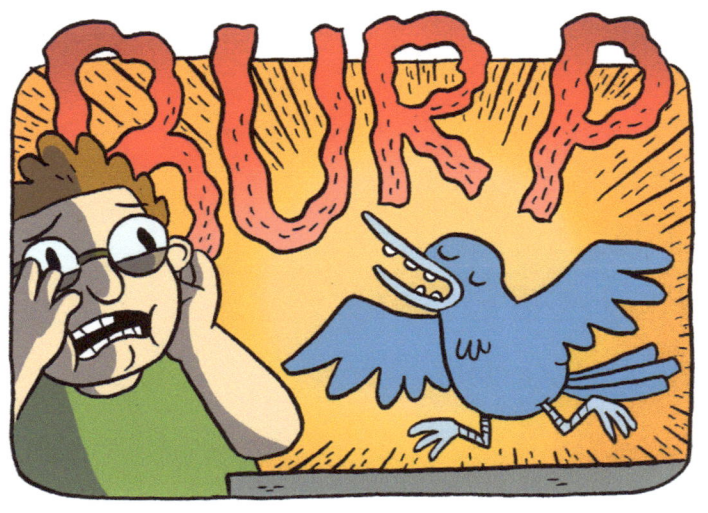

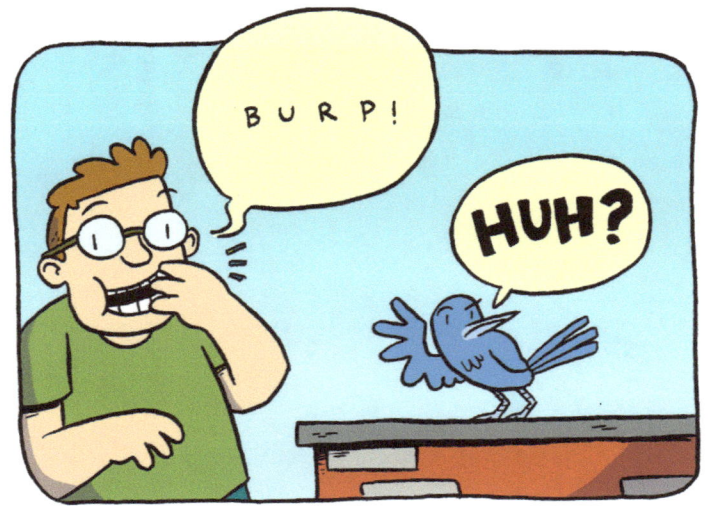

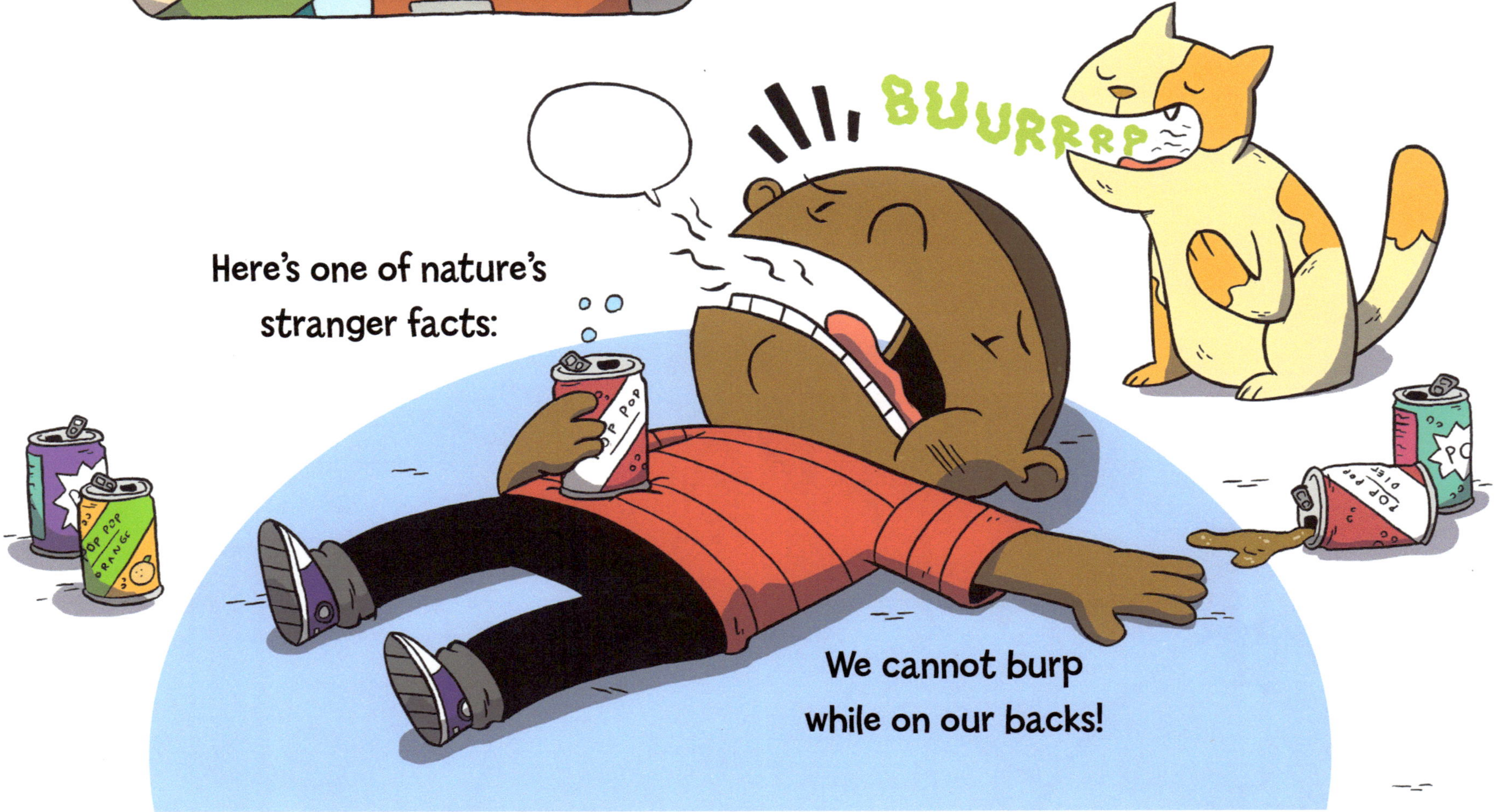

We cannot burp while on our backs!

Most critters will produce a fart.
Just a few cannot take part.

Jellyfish, sponges, anemones—
None of these can "cut the cheese"!

Who farts the most? Big surprise! The mightiest is mini-size.

From all the wood that termites chew, they far out-fart the cow or gnu.

Snakes "cut one" to drive away
A predator in search of prey.

Fish fart to communicate.
The bubbles help them congregate.

Farts escape when we're at rest.
A bedtime fart can't be suppressed.

And if your room is sealed up tight,
The fart may linger overnight.

Don't rip one in the elevator!

Do *you* fart often? The facts say
We average fourteen toots per day!

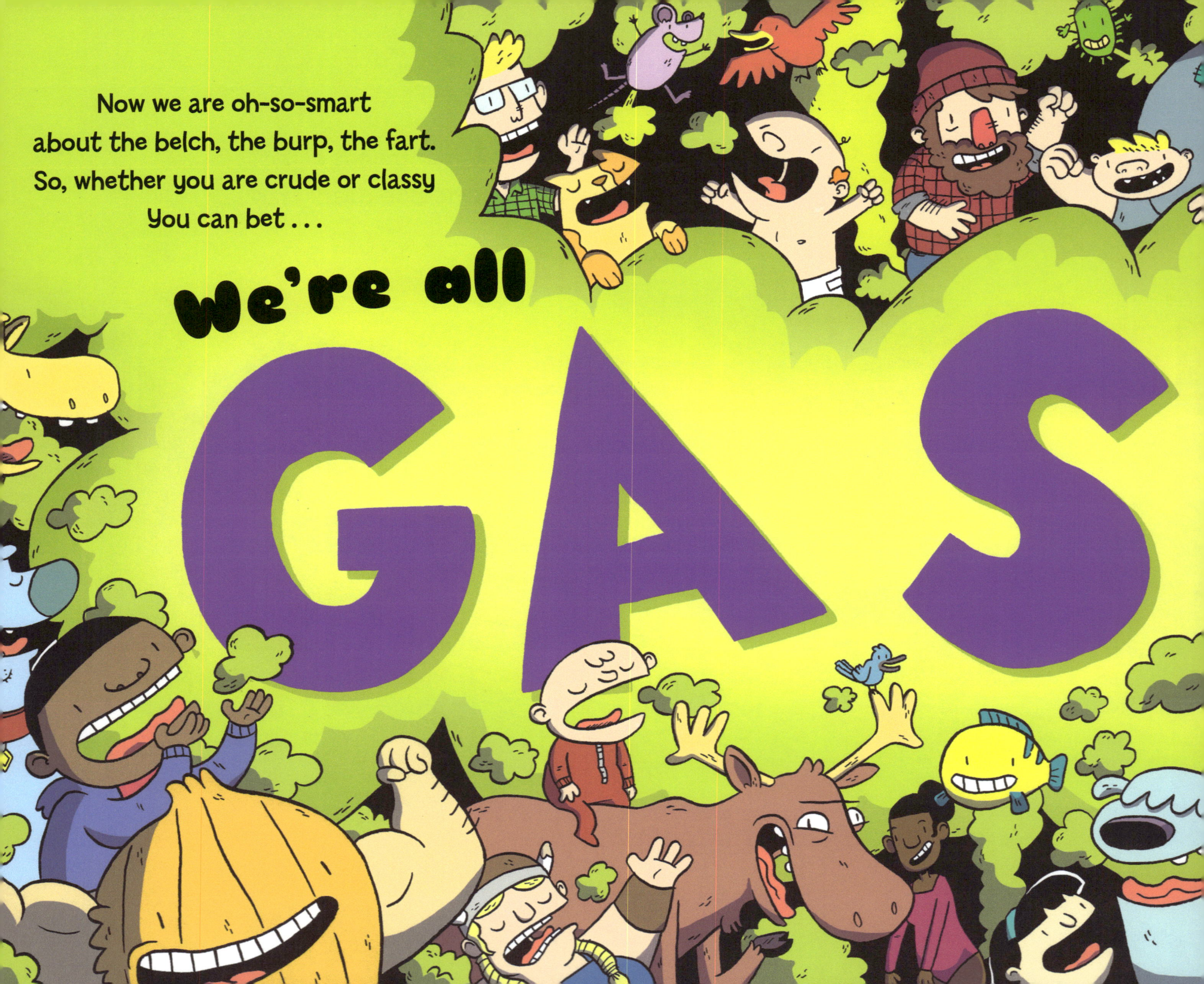

FART-TASTIC FACTS &

- The word "fart" comes from an Old English word, *feortan*. Experts say that *feortan* was meant to spell out what a fart sounds like.

  - Farts are intestinal gas. This gas comes from swallowed air that gets mixed with intestinal fluids, bacteria, and stomach acid. All combine in varying amounts to make a brew of pure P.U.!

- The scent of gas comes from hydrogen sulfide and other sulfur-containing components. Foods that have a lot of sulfur are cauliflower, eggs, and meat. All yummy (well, maybe not cauliflower), and all very stinky fart-producers!

  - Beans, bread, milk, raisins, cabbage, corn, and peppers are other fart-producing foods for most people.

- The longer you hold in a fart, the smellier it becomes. A withheld fart will absorb other gases before it finally passes.

  - The silent-but-deadly fart is a particularly stinky fart that arrives without any obvious noise. These are farts that tend to have more bacterial contribution and emerge as smaller, warm-and-smelly bubbles. No sound is needed to mark the arrival of an SBD fart!

- Humidity, temperature, wind speed and direction—these are all factors that determine how fast and far a fart will travel. Just ate a big bowl of cauliflower or a batch of eggs for breakfast? Hope and pray for a windy day and try to avoid elevators, small rooms, and car rides!

  - It takes about 13 to 20 seconds after it emerges for us to smell a fart. After that, farts aren't detectable for very long—just a few seconds for most of them.

- The term "morning thunder" refers to a particularly loud fart made soon after waking up.

  - A person can buy special underwear meant to absorb the smell of a fart. It is cheaper, though, just to walk away quickly or blame the dog.

- The official medical term for farting is "flatus."

  - A "whoopee cushion" is a rubber device (resembling a hot-water bottle) that makes a fart-like sound when sat upon. Pranksters hide it under a cushion as a gag.

- Dogs and cats + meat-rich diets = stinky pet farts!

  - Cows + lots of air for digestion = hours of noisy farts!

BURP-TACULAR BITS

- Farts are colorless, but they have inspired these colorful expressions: air attack, backdoor trumpet, bottom burp, Bronx cheer, cheek beep, colon cologne, cut the cheese, Dutch oven, let one rip, ringtailed roarer, step on a duck, talking pants, tooter, and whoever smelt it, dealt it.

  - Where do farts go? Fart gas mostly becomes part of the air or atmosphere of the area where the fart emerged.

- Burps come from the stomach. Farts come from the intestine. Burp gas is different than fart gas. Thank goodness!

  - What's the difference between a belch and a burp? Belches are generally stronger (in noise, force, duration) than burps. You would never belch the baby!

- Burp gas is fast! Burps travel a shorter, less complicated route to their exits than farts. It's stomach to esophagus to mouth to *brrrp!* There usually isn't enough time to cover your mouth before a burp shows up—but you can still say "Excuse me!" after the fact.

  - If you want to burp the alphabet—or your favorite song— you'll need to gulp in a lot of air first.

- If the gas could be collected, the burps of ten cows over a year's time could heat a small house for an entire year.

  - The loudest recorded burp is greater than the roar of a motorcycle!

- Because of the lack of gravity, a burp made while in outer space is likely to bring up some food as well. This is called a "wet burp."

  - The sound of a burp comes from the passing gas causing a small piece of cartilage that covers your wind-pipe (called the epiglottis) to snap and vibrate.

- A burp is mostly oxygen and nitrogen. Drinking soda adds carbon dioxide to the burpy mix.

  - The official medical term for belching is "eructation."

- Other words for burps and burping: organ recital, air biscuit, soda fart, gas-pression, reviewing the day's menu, belly bark.

Parting advice:
It's better to urp a burp and bear the shame
Than squelch a belch and bear the pain.

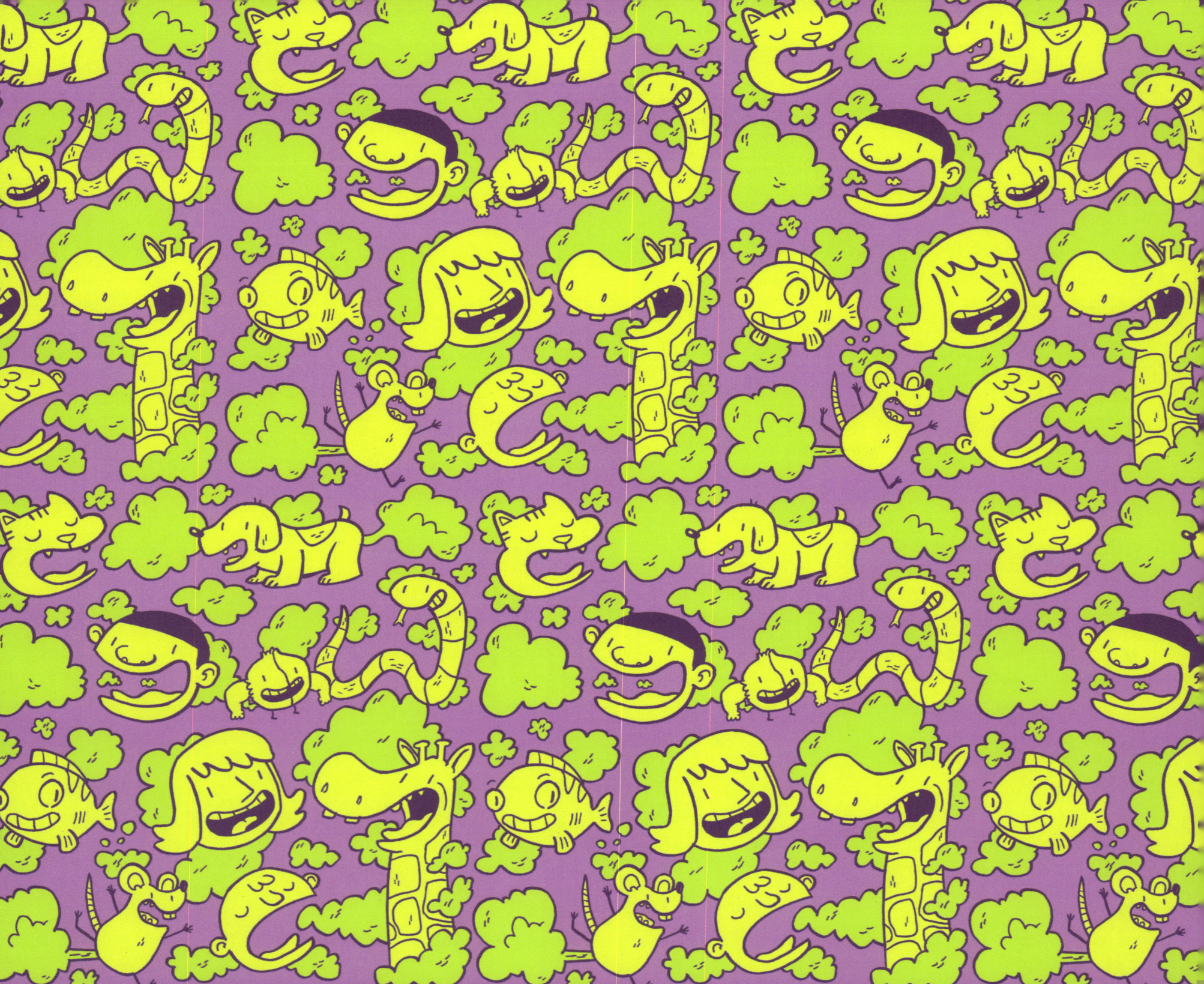

Artie Bennett is the highly acclaimed author of *The Butt Book*, *Poopendous!*, and *Peter Panda Melts Down!* His books have been lavished with praise, with *Poopendous!* receiving a Cybils Award nomination for Best Nonfiction Picture Book.

Visit www.ArtieBennett.com before someone else does!

Also by Artie Bennett

"You must immediately go and buy *Poopendous!* It appears there is no topic Mr. Bennett can't make funny and educational."
(The Huffington Post)

Pranas T. Naujokaitis is the epic-and-awesome creator of *The Totally Awesome Epic Quest of the Brave Boy Knight*, *The Radically Awesome Adventures of the Animal Princess*, and *Dinosaurs in Space*.

Mr. Naujokaitis ("no-you-kite-us"; see, it's not that hard!) did a lot of (very) personal research for *Belches, Burps, and Farts—Oh My!* and admits that, when accused, he tends to blame any evidence of flatulence on his cat.

Also by Pranas T. Naujokaitis

"Big-hearted fun [with] the power to please younger readers."
(Kirkus Reviews)

www.ingramcontent.com/pod-product-compliance
Lightning Source LLC
Chambersburg PA
CBHW041402080426

42696CB00049B/51